OVERCOMING THE STORMS OF LIFE

By
Billy Joe Daugherty

Copyright © 1991
Victory Christian Center
All rights reserved.
Printed in the U.S.A.

To reproduce this book in any form, please contact the author.

All Scriptures contained herein, unless otherwise noted, are from the New King James Version of the Bible, copyright 1979, 1980, 1982, Thomas Nelson, Inc., Publishers.

For more information about Pastors Billy Joe and Sharon Daugherty's books and tapes, write:

VICTORY CHRISTIAN CENTER
Information Services
7700 South Lewis
Tulsa, Oklahoma 74136-7700
To Order 1-888-874-8674
Prayer Line (918) 496-0700

ISBN No. 1-56267-006-9

Table of Contents

1 Why Do Storms Come? 1
2 Power to Overcome 2
3 Build Your House on the Rock 4
4 Key For Overcoming 5
5 Jesus Faced Storms 8
6 Releasing Your Faith 9
7 Count It All Joy 13
8 The Testing of Your Faith 14
9 Becoming a Doer of the Word 15
10 Agree With the Word 17
11 Leave the Past Behind 20
12 Praise Will Bring You Through 22
13 Don't Quit! 23
14 Hold Fast to the Confession of
   Your Faith... 25
15 Keep Your Eyes on the
   End Goal: JESUS! 26
   Personal Prayer of Commitment 28

1 Why Do Storms Come?

At some time in life, every person faces storms in the form of situations, circumstances, obstacles, problems and difficulties. The storms come to take you off the course God would have you run. They come to deter you and to literally keep you from being all God wants you to be, from having all God wants you to have and from doing all He wants you to do.

Sometimes the storms are from the devil. Sometimes they are related to other people - problems they are going through that affect you by your association with them. Sometimes you create our own storms by your own mistakes.

Most important to you is to know that you're going to make it and to know how to make it as an overcomer. The storms of life do not make you or break you. It is the Word of God working in your life that makes you victorious, and it is the loack of God's Word that makes people fail. The storm merely reveals whether you are a doer of the Word or just a hearer.

2 Power to Overcome

> Who shall separate us from the love of Christ? Shall tribulation, or distress, or persecution, or famine, or nakedness, or peril, or sword?
>
> As it is written: `For Your sake we are killed all day long; we are accounted as sheep for the slaughter.'
>
> Yet in all these things <u>we are more than conquerors through Him who loved us</u>.
>
> **Romans 8:35-37**

Paul was declaring that in any circumstance, we have the power to overcome. He also said:

> I know how to be abased, and I know how to abound. Everywhere and in all things I have learned both to be full and to be hungry, both to abound and to suffer need.
>
> I can do all things through Christ who strengthens me.
>
> **Philippians 4:12-13**

In other words, he was saying, "Circumstances don't dictate my life. What dominates me is what God has done in me and what He's yet doing for me."

To get through the storms of life, you need to know who you are in Christ, through what Jesus has done for you at Calvary, in the resurrection and in the sending of the Holy Spirit, and to know what He's doing right now at the right hand of the Father. Hebrews 7:25 says He's making daily intercession for you.

You may ask for prayer from other people, which is important. But there's one person you can count on who's praying for you and that is Jesus. He ever lives to make intercession for you. He's praying _for_ you, not against you! He's praying for you to win!

Believe you are going to get through the storm you are facing. Expect God to help you. He cares about your life.

What God did for the apostle Paul, He will do for you. Declare out loud, "I am more than a conqueror through Him that loved me." With faith say, "I can do all things through Christ who strengthens me."

3 Build Your House on the Rock

Therefore whoever <u>hears</u> these sayings of Mine, and <u>does</u> them, I will liken him to a wise man who built his house on the <u>rock</u>:

And the rain descended, the floods came, and the winds blew and beat on that house; and <u>it did not fall</u>, for it was founded on the rock.

Now everyone who <u>hears</u> these sayings of Mine, and <u>does not do them</u>, will be like a foolish man who built his house on the <u>sand</u>:

And the rain descended, the floods came, and the winds blew and beat on that house; and <u>it fell</u>. And great was its fall.

Matthew 7:24-27

The rains, winds and floods came against both houses. One was affected and the other wasn't. Jesus said all of us will encounter storms. Those who hear and do the Word of God will stand. Those who only hear but don't do the Word will fall. You decide whether you will stand or fall by what you do with God's Word.

4 Key For Overcoming

The key for overcoming is <u>doing the Word of God</u>. The wise man did the Word. Both the wise man and the foolish man heard the Word, but the wise man became a doer of the Word.

You'll be wise to become a doer of the Word that you know. You already know enough to put you over. If you simply do what you already know, you can be victorious in every area of your life. I am saying that for a reason, because many people improperly perceive that the solution to their problems is gaining more knowledge. In some cases, that may be true. But for the people who have heard the Word over a period of time, it's not necessarily more truth that they need, but it's the application of the truth they have already received.

Jesus didn't say the man who stood was the man who got more information. In fact, He says they both had the information. The overcomer was the one who took what he knew, applied it to the situation and put it into practice. He became a doer of the Word of God. In other words, there was a <u>corresponding action</u>.

> Now it happened, on a certain day, that He got into a boat with His disciples. And He said to them, `Let us go over to the other side of the lake.' And they launched out.
>
> But as they sailed He fell asleep. And a windstorm came down on the lake, and they were filling with water, and were in jeopardy.
>
> And they came to Him and awoke Him, saying, `Master, Master, we are perishing!' Then He arose and rebuked the wind and the raging of the water. And they ceased, and there was a calm.
>
> But He said to them, `<u>Where is your faith?</u>'And they were afraid, and marveled, saying to one another, `Who can this be? For He commands even the winds and water, and they obey Him!'
>
> Luke 8:22-25

Jesus asked the disciples, "Where is your faith?" All the disciples could see was disaster, problems and difficulties. Jesus didn't commend them for waking Him up! He stopped the storm, but in essence, it was a rebuke! He said, "Where is your faith?" In other words, Jesus was saying, "You already have the faith to stop the storm and get through it. Why didn't you use it? Where is your faith?"

They had the ability to use their faith, but they didn't. Faith and fear repel each other. They're opposites. If fear rises up, faith goes out the door. If faith rises up, fear goes out the door. That's the key to coming through your storms: <u>being a doer of the Word by releasing your faith and dispelling the fear</u>.

Fear paralyzes while faith activates. When you believe what God says and stand on it, fear will leave you. But when you believe the circumstances and words the devil brings, then faith will leave.

Choose to believe the Word and doubt the lies of the enemy.

5 Jesus Faced Storms

If you're living for Christ, you've taken a stand against the devil. This means you'll encounter him head on. Wherever Paul preached and ministered, he was opposed. Jesus, from His very first message, was criticized and ridiculed. In fact, in His first hometown sermon, they tried to throw Him off a cliff and kill Him. That was just the beginning of opposition He encountered. Everywhere He went, Jesus faced storms: criticism, slander, and wrong words spoken about Him. If Jesus overcame all these storms, so can you because He lives in you.

Sometimes the storm people face is sickness or disease that tries to rob them of health. Sometimes it's a financial storm. You add up the bills and they exceed the income. Then there's a storm of worry and anxiety that tries to come against you over a family dispute.

Some face storms related to a relationship problem, with difficulties and misunderstandings in which people say critical things. Thank God, you and I are going to get through these storms.

Jesus lives in you by faith. Believe He is in you now and expect Him to help you overcome every storm through the faith He has given you.

6 Releasing Your Faith

Here are three primary ways to release your faith.

Believe the Word

You release your faith by what you believe in your heart.

Romans 10:17 says, "**So then faith comes by hearing, and hearing by the word of God.**" When you hear the Word of the Lord, you believe it. Faith rises up. Faith is the substance of things you have hoped for. It's the evidence of things you cannot see. It's the title deed that you hold concerning those things which are unseen. You know you have them, because God's Word promises them to you.

Speak the Word

You release your faith by the words you speak. Second Corinthians 4:13 describes the "spirit of faith." "**But since we have the same spirit of faith, according to what is written, `I believed and therefore I spoke,' we also believe and therefore speak.**" The spirit of faith is believing and speaking according to that which God has spoken.

To get through the storms, you need to train your tongue to speak the right things when there's no storm. It is difficult to lasso your tongue and wrestle it under control after the storm hits. When the storm hits, many people run their mouth 90 miles an hour with doubt, unbelief, disaster, calamity and tragedy. Everything the doctors have said they repeat verbatim as if it came straight from God. Everything the world has said they pronounce as if it's an edict from Jesus Himself.

Isaiah said, **"Who has believed our report?"** (Isaiah 53:1). You must discipline your tongue to speak God's report. Proverbs 18:21 says, **"Death and life are in the power of the tongue..."** Proverbs 6:2 says, **"You are snared by the words of your own mouth; you are taken by the words of your mouth."**

Jesus said, **"...For out of the abundance of the heart the mouth speaks"** (Matthew 12:34). Get a hold on your tongue now! Make a decision that you're going to speak what God's Word says.

Jesus said to Peter, **"...Indeed, Satan has asked for you, that he may sift you as wheat"** (Luke 22:31).

I believe that's a revelation for every believer, that Satan is going to sift and find out what's really inside of us. According to Matthew 7, the storm is going to come against everyone. It's going to sift. What is deep on the inside of you will surface when the storm hits.

We have people in our ministry and some of our church members who've gone through terrible financial storms. We've had an opportunity to pray with many of them. In one instance, the man said over and over, "I'm going to make it." It looked like the whole world was going to crash in. Problem after problem came, but he said, "I'm going to make it." HE DID!

When the storm is raging, pick your nose up out of the water and breathe! Just hang on to what God has said and declare it out loud. Everything within your feeling realm may want to say what it looks like, but faith refuses to bow its knee to the system of this world. Faith won't compromise. It just keeps speaking what God said.

Psalm 112:7-8 say that the man whose heart is fixed (steadfast) will not be moved when evil tidings come.

> **He will not be afraid of evil tidings; his heart is steadfast, trusting in the Lord.**

His heart is established; he will not be
afraid....

When the evil report comes, if your heart is settled on what you believe, you can say, "My God is able. It is well with my soul."

Act on the Word

<u>The third part of releasing your faith is acting upon what God says</u>. There's a corresponding action with everything you're speaking. You have to act like the Word is true.

How would the disciples have acted in the midst of the storm? They would have awakened Jesus and said, "Jesus, we're going to stop this storm. Do You want to watch us?"

They could have stood up in the boat and acted on what they believed. As you begin to act on what you believe, God will give you specific direction of the corresponding action. It may not always be the same thing. It is Spirit-directed faith.

The Israelites had to listen for God's direction in every battle they faced. In taking Jericho, they had to march around the city once a day for six days and seven times on the seventh day (Joshua 6:1-5). That was their act of faith. But in the next city, the action of faith was different.

7 Count It All Joy

I think James had terrific insight about coming through battles and storms. He said, **"My brethren, count it all joy when you fall into various trials"** (James 1:2).

What do you think that means? It means, "Get joyful when you encounter various trials, difficulties and temptations." If you read this with natural eyes rather than with spiritual eyes, you'll really miss the point. Nehemiah 8:10 says, **"...for the joy of the Lord is your strength."**

What happens when you lose your joy? You lose your strength. Without strength, you can't overcome the adversity. So what did James say? When you encounter a storm, then start rejoicing, not for the storm, but rejoice that <u>God is with you</u>.

Paul said, **"Rejoice in the Lord always. Again I will say, rejoice!"** (Philippians 4:4).

He wrote this word from prison! Imagine someone in chains encouraging others to rejoice. Paul had learned the secret of Victory - joy.

Faith is joyful - so **<u>Rejoice</u>**.

8 The Testing of Your Faith

Knowing that the testing of your faith produces patience.

But let patience have its perfect work, that you may be perfect and complete, lacking nothing.

James 1:3-4

What is the end result of being steadfast? You come through the storm. The end result of not giving up is you get to the other side! James is saying, Let patience have its <u>completed work</u> or <u>end result</u>.

Let your steadfast attitude work its way all the way to the end so you'll be perfect or complete, entire, lacking nothing. *Perfect* means "complete, matured, or entire." You'll grow up in the fullness of Jesus Christ and you'll lack nothing. The end of the storm is in this verse: <u>perfect and entire, wanting nothing.</u> David said, **"I would have lost heart, unless I had believed that I would see the goodness of the Lord in the land of the living"** (Psalm 27:13). He was saying, "If I hadn't had a vision of the end of this thing, I'd have given up and quit."

9 Becoming a Doer of the Word

James 1:22 says, "But be doers of the word, and not hearers only, deceiving yourselves." He comes back to the words of Jesus. This is Matthew 7:24 repeated in a little different form. James says, "But be doers of the word, and not hearers only, deceiving yourselves."

Someone who just hears the teaching of the Word, but doesn't apply it to their circumstances is self-deceived, because they think since they've heard the message it's going to work. It doesn't work because you've heard it. It works because you apply it! It's like Windex. It doesn't clean the windows in the bottle. You have to spray it on, and then you have to rub the window until it's spotless.

Just because you've got God's Word inside of you doesn't mean it's going to do the work. You have to apply it to each situation. Don't just be a hearer. Be a doer of God's Word.

James 1:23-24 say:

> For if anyone is a hearer of the Word and not a doer, he is like a man observing his natural face in a mirror;

> For he observes himself, goes away, and immediately forgets what kind of man he was.

He looks in the mirror and sees the mirror of God's Word. The Bible is referred to as a mirror. It gives the image of God inside of us. When we look into the Word, we see who we really are in Him. We see the new creation God has made us to be in Christ Jesus.

Whoever looks into the Word and is just a hearer and not a doer, forgets who he really is. On Sunday in your church, you say, "I'm more than a conqueror." On Monday the storm comes. You'd better look in the mirror again! Say it out loud, "I'm more than a conqueror."

10 Agree With the Word

When circumstances come, are you going to say what the circumstances say or what the Word says?

Here's the real battle. Some people say, "If I say what the Word says, I'll be lying." It all depends upon what you call truth. If you call the circumstances of the world a greater truth than God's Word, then in your own perspective, it would be lying. But if you get a revelation that God's Word is greater than all circumstances, His Word will remain when the whole world is burned up.

Lock into the Word. Jesus said, **"Heaven and earth will pass away, but My word will by no means pass away"** (Matthew 24:35).

When you begin to understand the permanency of the Word, then you'll understand that when you're saying what the Word says, you're not lying. You'll finally start telling the truth!

As long as you speak your feelings, that's the way it's going to be. But if you'll speak God's Word, it'll lift you up to be what it says. You have to keep looking at the mirror of the Word.

That's why Joshua 1:8 says, **"This Book of the Law shall not depart from your mouth, but you shall meditate in it day and night...."**

Rise early and meditate on what the Word of God says about you: "I have the mind of Christ. I have the wisdom of God. Christ dwells in me through the power of the Holy Spirit." As you speak the Word, the reality of it will begin to take place.

Some have said, "Well, I said it three times and it didn't work. I confessed all my needs were met last week and the money didn't come. I'm giving up on that stuff!" There's more to it than just saying it for a little while. I'm talking about committing your heart to the Word of God and becoming locked into it.

Take the attitude if it doesn't work for anyone else in the entire world, it's going to work for me. I am not basing my faith on the Word's fulfillment in any other person's life. People say, "I know So-and-so, Reverend So-and-so, Aunt So-and-so, or Grandma So-and-so. They were good Christians and they believed the Word, but it didn't happen to them."

I'm not their judge, so I can't say anything about it. I wasn't there. I don't know the situation. But I do know, "God is not a man, that He should lie, nor a son of man, that He should repent. Has He said, and will He not do it? Or has He spoken, and will He not make it good?" (Numbers 23:19).

We've got to get to the point where we just say, "The Word is true. The Word works." We must work the Word and let it work in us.

Don't Be Critical of Others

You can negate the power of God with your words. One of the things you have to watch in the storms is keeping your tongue from speaking evil about someone else. If you get into judgment and criticism, you can become an attacker of others in your storm. It can rob you of your own faith. That's why Jesus spoke about forgiveness after speaking on mountain-moving faith.

> And whenever you stand praying, if you have anything against anyone, forgive him, that your Father in heaven may also forgive you your trespasses.
>
> But if you do not forgive, neither will your Father in heaven forgive your trespasses."
>
> **Mark 11:25-26**

11 Leave the Past Behind

Do not remember the former things, nor consider the things of old.
Isaiah 43:18

To get through your storms, you'll have to forget about your past experiences. You'll have to let go of those things which are behind you.

As a baseball player in the position of short stop, let's assume you miss a ground ball and you miss the throw to first base. The worst thing you can do is kick the ground and worry about your errors. Why? Because there's another ball coming! If your mind is on the last mistake, you'll never be able to handle the next situation. You'll commit the same error.

This happened in the 1990 College World Series. An outstanding third baseman who had the lowest error percentage of all the third basemen in the nation committed three errors in a row. They had to pull him from the game, because he got his mind on the errors, and he kept making the same mistake over and over.

We can't always explain why something doesn't happen, but one thing we can do is ask for the grace of God to forget about it and leave it with God. There are other relatives, other situations, other circumstances and other battles that you're going to have to face, and you need all of your energy focused on them rather than dwelling on your past.

> **But he who looks into the perfect law of liberty and continues in it, and is not a forgetful hearer but a doer of the work, <u>this one will be blessed in what he does</u>.**
>
> **James 1:25**

This is the person whose house will stand in the storm. The blessing of God comes to those who don't forget the Word, but rather continue to do it.

Keep the eyes of your heart focused on God's Word. You will not be disappointed.

12 Praise Will Bring You Through

It was praise that brought Paul and Silas through the Philippian jail storm. They had been beaten and were thrown in prison and bound in stocks, but at midnight, they began to sing and praise the Lord. They not only were released but led the jailor and his family to Jesus.

Don't lose your song of praise in the storm. Force yourself to praise God. There are times when you're going to have to make a decision to dance before the Lord. Your old body will say, "Lay down. You're a hypocrite. You're not praising God."

Your mind may tell you, "Your heart's not really in this." Your heart can be into praise and worship before your mind and body are! Your heart knows what's right, so make your body and your mind do what you ought to do.

"In everything give thanks: for this is the will of God in Christ Jesus concerning you" (1 Thessalonians 5:18).

Put on your garment of praise and put off that spirit of heaviness.

13 Don't Quit!

...in due season we shall reap if we do not lose heart.

Galatians 6:9

You will receive a harvest. You will see the end result if you don't quit and if you don't throw in the towel saying, "I've tried this long enough."

Look at it this way. What have you got to go back to? People who are delivered from drugs and alcohol say, "Boy, I've really been going through a storm. My body wants a fix so bad. I need a drink. The struggle of getting out of drugs and alcohol is so terrible." What's worse is going back and becoming a slave to that stuff again and getting back into those chains.

You'll have to go through your storms. Jesus had to get through His storm, because there was a demon-possessed man on the other side. In most cases, the storm comes *to stop you from reaching the goals God has for you. It comes to get you to give up. It comes to get you to take an easier pathway that's not as difficult so you'll miss the plan of God.*

The devil is a cunning, clever schemer. He realizes God is moving on the earth through the Holy Spirit, imparting divine direction to His servants on the earth and telling them what to do. Therefore, if he can distract God's servants from doing His will, he will abort and stop God's plan in the earth.

That's exactly what happened to Adam and Eve in the garden. God intended to rule the earth through Adam and Eve. Satan came to get them off track and turn them away. His strategy hasn't changed. He's coming against you for the same purpose.

Now, the storms will come, but just because you have problems doesn't mean you're not in the will of God. I've rejoiced in that thought many times in my life. "Oh, God, I thank You that I'm in Your will."

Stay with it. Keep believing God. Continue speaking the Word. The harvest you will reap is worth the price you have to pay to get it.

14 Hold Fast to the Confession of Your Faith

Hebrews 10:23 says, "Let us hold fast the profession of our faith without wavering; (for he is faithful that promised)" (KJ). Hold fast to the confession or the words of your lips, without wavering, concerning what God has spoken to you. Wavering means to go back and forth.

Just because you don't understand something doesn't mean you can't believe in God or that His Word isn't working. We don't all understand how a little seed put into the ground pops through the earth, but farmers believe it because they've seen it year after year. It's the same way with God's Word. Hold fast to your planting of the Word (the seed), for it will produce a harvest.

<u>Therefore do not cast away your confidence, which has great reward.</u>

For you have need of endurance, so that after you have done the will of God, you may receive the promise.

Hebrews 10:35-36

15 Keep Your Eyes on the End Goal: JESUS!

When you're weary and the storm has been going on a long time, set your eyes upon Jesus.

> <u>Looking unto Jesus</u>, the author and finisher of our faith, who for the joy that was set before Him endured the cross, despising the shame, and has sat down at the right hand of the throne of God.
>
> Hebrews 12:2

God is saying to us that we shouldn't be overly concerned about the obstacles we're going through. Look what Jesus had to go through to reach His goal. Keep your eyes on the end goal. His name is JESUS! We're not just going toward a thing. We're going toward a person. We're going toward the fulfillment of His will in our lives. We're going toward the completion of His plans for us.

Isaiah 40:31 says:

> <u>But those who wait on the Lord shall renew their strength; they shall mount up with wings like eagles, they shall run and not be weary, they shall walk and not faint.</u>

Those who are waiting upon the Lord will not quit! Waiting upon the Lord is ministering unto Him, serving, blessing, praising and worshipping Him and waiting in His presence. As you minister to the Lord, He imparts strength to you.

An eagle rides above a storm. It's time that we mount up with wings as eagles and take hold of God's power, strength and grace. It's time to begin to praise and worship and thank Him, no matter what the storm, no matter what the obstacle, no matter how you've been defeated or failed in the past. We've all faced it. We've all missed it. Let go of it now and leave it behind.

Let's go on with God, rising above every storm you now face or you'll ever face. Let's ride on the winds of the Spirit, like the eagle! Hallelujah!

I pray for the Father to strengthen and encourage you to the point that you're fully confident that no matter what storm you face, you're coming through to victory in the name of Jesus.

The strategy for getting through your storms is in the Word of God. I pray that God will give you a greater hunger and thirst for His Word.

Personal Prayer of Commitment

Father, I desire to make a fresh commitment to You today. I believe Jesus Christ is Your Son and that He died and was resurrected to bring forth new life. I renounce the works of the devil in my life. I accept Jesus Christ as my personal Lord and Savior today.

Empower me with Your Holy Spirit, Father, that I'll not only be able to stand in the storms of life, but I'll soar above them in Your strength.

Father, have Your way in my life beginning today. I yield completely to Your plan and Your will, for You've said in Your Word that Your plans are to prosper me and give me hope and a future (Jeremiah 29:11, NIV).

With Your help, Lord, I'll not quit. I'll make no plans to fail. Today is a new day. The storms of life will not weaken me, but with my eyes upon You, Lord Jesus, I'll overcome and be strengthened. Amen.

Signature

Date

OTHER BOOKS BY BILLY JOE DAUGHERTY

BB01	This New Life	.50
BB02	Absolute Victory	2.50
BB03	Faith Power	3.95
BB04	Death Is Not the End	.50
BB05	Be On Fire For the Lord	.50
BB06	The Fear of the Lord	.50
BB07	Demonstration of the Gospel	4.50
BB08	Diligence Produces Results	.50
BB09	Exceedingly Abundantly	.50
BB10	You Are Valuable	.50
BB12	You Can Be Healed	5.95
BB13	Building Stronger Marriages and Families	6.95
BB14	You Can Start Over	.50

BOOKS BY SHARON DAUGHERTY

BS01	A Fruitful Life, Walking in the Spirit	3.95
BS02	Called By His Side	3.00

To Order:

VICTORY CHRISTIAN CENTER
Information Services
7700 South Lewis
Tulsa, Oklahoma 74136-7700
To Order 1-888-874-8674
Prayer Line (918) 496-0700